Dan Cannon

Mountain Man of God

A Devotional Guide for Men

Mountain Man of God – A Devotional Guide for Men

All scripture quotes are from the New International Version of the Bible.

ISBN 979-8-9998877-9-5

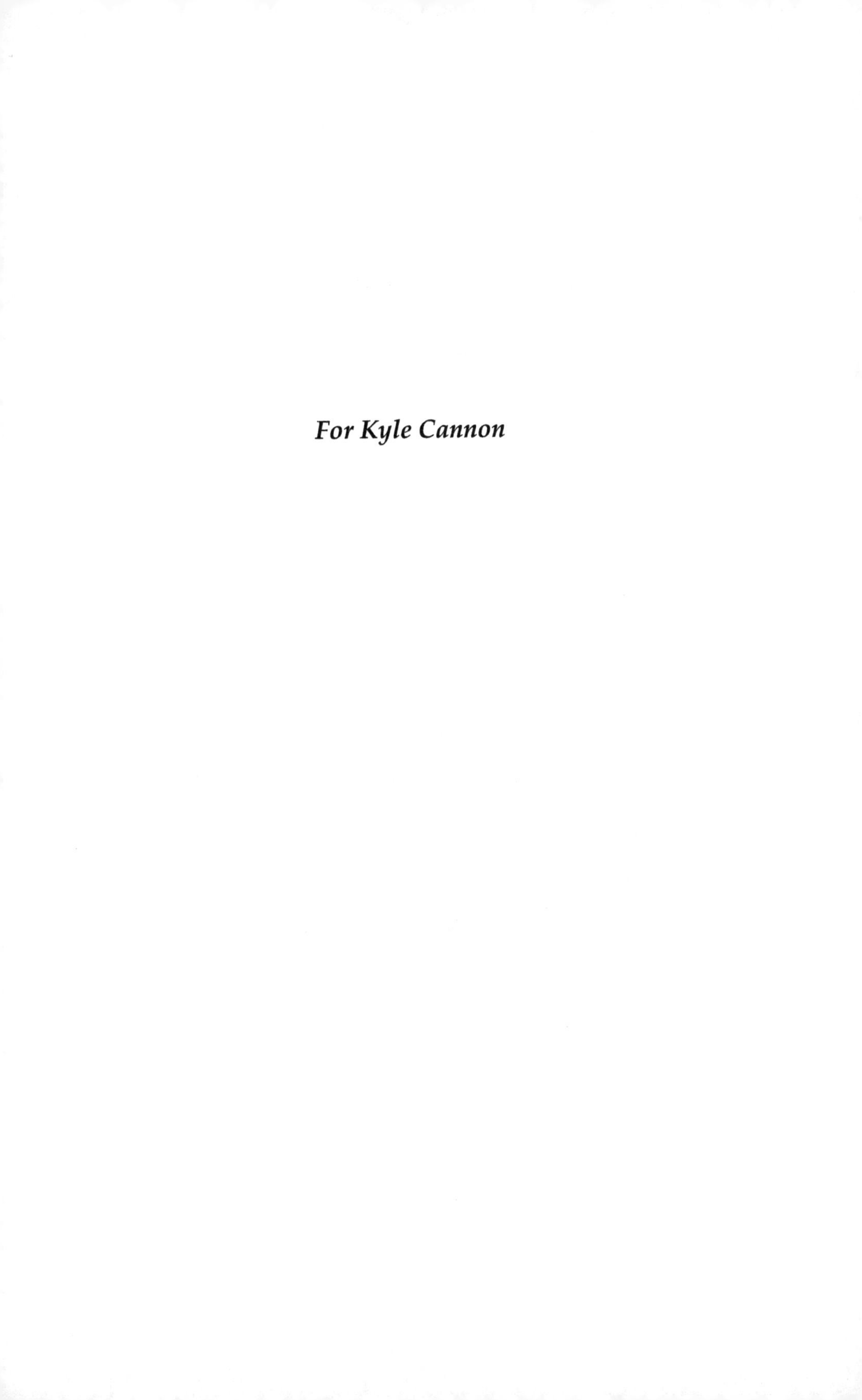

For Kyle Cannon

This Devotional Guide belongs to:

____

But you, man of God, flee from all this,
and pursue righteousness, godliness,
faith, love, endurance and gentleness.
1 Timothy 6:11

Introduction

I chose to name this devotional guide, *Mountain Man of God,* to evoke themes of strength, solitude, and spirituality, conjuring images of resilience and faith in a rugged, natural setting. Not that all of us live in the mountains. Mountains can be symbolic of the rugged terrain of daily life that we all experience. And, as we walk in our faith each day, we sometimes face mountain-like challenges. God offers to us the strength, wisdom, and faith to overcome these 'mountains', all to His glory. I also chose the name to attract those drawn to personal growth, faith journeys, or outdoor adventure with a spiritual focus.

We'll explore themes of gratitude, faith, patience, generosity, kindness, trust, hope, humility, and joy – all accompanied by scripture. As this is a devotional guide, there is room for you to reflect on your wins, your struggles, your fears, and the things and people you are grateful for each day.

Know that as a Mountain Man of God, you are the fire that warms a room, the heart that beats boldly and humbly, the courage that stands fully in God's light. To be a Mountain Man of God is to carry his love within you, a steady source of generosity, strength, and faith.

But being a Mountain Man of God is not about performance. It is about authenticity.

This guide is your space to explore what it means to grow more deeply as a man, not as a character, not as a role, but as your true, spiritual self. It is a place to more deeply connect with your faith and life path.

There will be days when your spiritual fire feels dimmed by doubt, comparison, or exhaustion. That is natural. Even the Sun sets only to rise again. So does the Mountain Man of God.

This devotional guide invites you to:

- Deepen your faith
- Express yourself honestly
- Lay down all burdens before the Lord
- Fully live your faith
- Trust in the Lord with all your heart

You are not here to wither.

You are here to grow and shine.

Let this be the space where you do exactly that.

How to Use This Devotional Guide

This guide is not meant to be rushed. It is meant to be lived in.

You may move through it in order or go to a page that calls to you. Some days you will reflect and pray boldly. Other days, you may just quietly ponder. Your devotional time and path has no wrong way.

The sections and prompts that follow are designed to guide you through different dimensions of your spiritual journey.

This devotional guide is not about becoming someone else. It is about deepening the faith you have and live by, and remembering who you already are. A *Mountain Man of God*.

Shine boldly.

Gratitude

Give thanks in all circumstances; for this is God's will for you in Christ Jesus.
1 Thessalonians 5:18

1 Thessalonians 5:18 (NIV) is short, direct, and worth deeper reflection: *"Give thanks in all circumstances; for this is God's will for you in Christ Jesus."*

Paul wrote these words to a young church navigating real hardship, not from a comfortable distance, but as someone who knew difficulty firsthand. And what he asks of them is striking. He doesn't say give thanks for all circumstances. He says give thanks in them. It's a small word, but it makes all the difference.

This isn't a call to pretend that hard seasons aren't hard, or to paste a smile over genuine pain. It's something deeper, a posture of the heart that remains anchored in gratitude regardless of what life looks like on any given day. In good times and hard times. When things make sense and when they don't.

Paul ties this gratitude directly to our relationship with Christ Jesus, not to favorable conditions, not to how we happen to feel on a particular morning. That's what makes it sustainable. After all, circumstances change. Emotions come and go. But Christ Jesus doesn't.

That's the invitation here. Not a checklist item, but a way of living: grounded, grateful, and rooted in something that nothing can touch.

Think back to a hard period of your life, a time when giving thanks felt less like a spiritual discipline and more like a contradiction, and, looking back now, where do you see God's hand in it?

What are three things, they don't have to be profound, that you can give thanks for today?

Let the peace of Christ rule in your hearts, since as members of one body you were called to peace. And be thankful. Let the message of Christ dwell among you richly as you teach and admonish one another with all wisdom through psalms, hymns, and songs from the Spirit, singing to God with gratitude in your hearts. And whatever you do, whether in word or deed, do it all in the name of the Lord Jesus, giving thanks to God the Father through him.

Colossians 3:15-17

Take a moment with Colossians 3:15-17 (NIV), because there's a lot packed into these three verses. Paul instructs believers to let the peace of Christ *rule* in their hearts, to let the message of Christ *dwell* among them richly, and to do everything, everything, in the name of the Lord Jesus, giving thanks to God the Father through Him.

The word rule is worth pausing on. Paul is saying that Christ's peace is meant to function foundationally inside us. When anxiety creeps in, when disagreements arise, when decisions need to be made, Christ's peace is our base and has the final say.

And then there's the word dwell. Not visit. Not make an occasional appearance. *Dwell,* as in, settle in, make yourself at home, fill the place up. Paul wants the message of Christ to be so thoroughly at home in the community of believers that it shapes their conversations, their worship, their teaching, and their everyday interactions with one another.

What strikes me most, though, is how many times gratitude shows up across just three verses. It isn't an afterthought or a footnote. Thankfulness is the atmosphere Paul is describing, the air that a Christ-based community breathes, together, every day.

After all, when Christ's peace is ruling your heart and His word is richly at home in your life, gratitude isn't something you have to manufacture. It's simply what spills out.

What is one choice you can make today to let the peace of Christ have the final say, over the worry, the frustration, or whatever else is competing for that space in your heart?

Gratitude and wisdom have a way of multiplying when they're passed along. Who in your family or community might benefit from you sharing something of what you're learning?

Think back to a moment when a song or an act of worship did something in you that words alone hadn't quite managed. What was it, and what might it tell you about your own heart?

Do not be anxious about anything, but in every situation, by prayer and petition, with thanksgiving, present your requests to God.
Philippians 4:6

Philippians 4:6 (NIV) doesn't ease you into it. It opens with a sweeping, unqualified command: *"Do not be anxious about anything."* Anything. Not most things. Not the smaller worries you can manage on your own. Anything.

What makes this even more remarkable is where Paul was when he wrote it — in prison. He wasn't offering this from a safe, comfortable place. He was writing from a cell, facing genuine uncertainty, and yet his counsel to the church at Philippi is unwavering: don't be anxious. Bring it to God instead.

And the remedy he offers is just as sweeping as the prohibition. *In every situation,* the mirror image of "anything", prayer, petition, and thanksgiving. No concern too small, no burden too heavy. All of it goes to God.

And Paul includes thanksgiving right there alongside prayer and petition. Not as a polite formality, but as something essential. Because thanksgiving reflects a particular kind of trust, the kind that brings a request to God and, in the very act of asking, acknowledges that He is already sovereign over whatever you're carrying. You're not informing God of a problem He missed. You're placing it in hands that were already holding it.

That's the reframe Paul is offering here. Anxiety isn't simply a feeling to be managed, it's an invitation. An invitation to pray, to ask, and to do both with a grateful and trusting heart.

What is the worry that's been sitting heaviest on you lately, the one you keep holding onto instead of handing over. How might you bring it to God today, with an open hand and a thankful heart?

Take a moment and put it into words a simple, honest prayer that names what you're carrying, asks God for what you need, and closes with gratitude for His presence and a care that never wavers.

Enter his gates with thanksgiving and his courts with praise; give thanks to him and praise his name.
Psalm 100:4

Psalm 100:4 (NIV) paints a picture that would have been immediately vivid to its original audience: *"Enter his gates with thanksgiving and his courts with praise; give thanks to him and praise his name."*

For the people of Israel, this wasn't abstract imagery. The gates and courts of the Jerusalem temple were real places, places you walked through, one after another, moving deliberately deeper into the presence of God. And what the psalmist is saying is that the way you walk through those gates matters. You don't shuffle in distracted or wander in indifferent. You come in with thanksgiving. You move deeper with praise.

There's an intentionality here. The progression from gates to courts isn't incidental. It describes a journey, a conscious, purposeful movement toward God, and thanksgiving and praise aren't simply nice accompaniments to that journey. They are the journey. They are how you draw near.

It's also worth noting that thanksgiving and praise appear twice in a single verse. The psalmist is making sure we don't treat gratitude as optional, or as a warm-up before the real worship begins. Gratitude *is* the worship. It is the fitting and natural response of anyone who has paused long enough to consider who God actually is and what He has actually done.

After all, when you truly know the Shepherd, the Creator, the one God, thanksgiving isn't something you have to work up. It's simply what comes out when you enter His presence.

When you think about drawing near to God, not as a religious routine but as a genuine, intentional movement toward Him, how do you walk through that door with thanksgiving already in your heart?

If gratitude shaped the first few minutes of your day instead of the headlines or your to-do list, how might that impact everything that follows?

Faith

Now faith is confidence in what we hope for and assurance about what we do not see.
Hebrews 11:1

If you were going to define faith in a single sentence, you'd be hard pressed to do better than Hebrews 11:1 (NIV): *"Now faith is confidence in what we hope for and assurance about what we do not see."*

Simple. Precise. And worth reflecting on.

The letter was written to Jewish Christians who were under real pressure, not the abstract, theological kind, but the kind that comes from family, community, and tradition pulling hard in the other direction to go back to the old ways. Return to what's familiar. Return to what you can see. And into that pressure, the writer of Hebrews firmly plants this definition of faith.

Note the word *confidence*. Not wishful thinking. Not a fragile, fingers-crossed kind of hope that evaporates the moment circumstances turn difficult. Confidence: settled, grounded, unwavering. Biblical faith, the writer is telling us, isn't a leap into the dark. It's a firm standing on something solid: the character of God and the reliability of His promises.

And then there's that second phrase: *assurance about what we do not see*. Faith operates beyond the boundaries of what can be observed, measured, or verified by human senses. That's not a weakness. That's the point. It's a Spirit-given capacity to perceive and rest in realities that are more certain than anything we can see, precisely because they rest on God Himself.

What follows this verse, of course, is one of the great galleries of Scripture: Abel, Noah, Abraham, Moses, and so many others. Each one a living illustration of exactly this kind of faith. Confident. Forward-looking. Anchored in what cannot be seen, but never in doubt about what cannot be shaken.

Think back to a time when you had no choice but to trust God for something completely outside your ability to see, control, or predict. Reflect on what that time did to your faith.

And in the everyday, the routine decision, the quiet uncertainty, how do you actually live as someone who is genuinely assured of what cannot yet be seen?

For we live by faith, not by sight.
2 Corinthians 5:7

Sometimes the most powerful things are said in the fewest words. 2 Corinthians 5:7 (NIV) is a perfect example: *"For we live by faith, not by sight."*

Only a few words. And yet there's an entire way of life contained in them.

Paul wrote this in the middle of a deeply personal reflection on suffering, mortality, and the hope of what lies ahead. He's not writing from a place of easy comfort, he rarely was. And yet his conclusion is this quiet, unshakeable declaration: we live by faith, not by sight.

The word *live* is worth deeper reflection. In the original Greek it carries the sense of walk: not a single moment of decision, but a continuous, day-by-day, step-by-step way of moving through life. Faith, Paul is telling us, isn't something you exercise once and then set aside. It's the ongoing manner in which Christians navigate everything.

And *not by sight,* that's the honest acknowledgment that what we can see, touch, and measure doesn't always tell the full story. Circumstances can look bleak and still be held within a purpose far greater than what's visible. Seasons can feel like endings that are actually beginnings.

The visible is real, but it isn't the whole picture.

What Paul is inviting us into is a countercultural way of living, one where confidence isn't anchored in how things look on any given day, but in the unseen, unchanging promises of a God who has never once failed to come through.

After all, sight is temporary. Faith is what carries you through.

Think back to a time when the visible circumstances were telling one story and faith was asking you to trust a different one entirely. What made that hard, and what did you learn from it?

And right now, in whatever you're currently facing, how do you take the next step by faith rather than waiting until you can see exactly where it leads.

For it is by grace you have been saved, through faith—and this is not from yourselves, it is the gift of God—not by works, so that no one can boast.

Ephesians 2:8-9

There are verses in Scripture that immediately impact me, and Ephesians 2:8-9 (NIV) is one of them: *"For it is by grace you have been saved, through faith — and this is not from yourselves, it is the gift of God — not by works, so that no one can boast."*

To fully appreciate what Paul is saying here, you need to back up a few verses. He's just finished describing humanity's natural condition in the starkest possible terms: dead in sin, following the ways of the world, objects of wrath. It's not a flattering picture. And then, right into that darkness, comes this.

By grace. Not by effort. Not by religious achievement. Not by being good enough, trying hard enough, or checking the right boxes. By grace, freely given, entirely unearned, originating wholly with God.

And then Paul says something else very impactful: faith, he says, is *not from yourselves*. It is completely the gift of God.

I find that both humbling and deeply freeing. Because if salvation were even partly our doing, we'd spend our lives wondering if we'd done enough. But if it is entirely God's work, from beginning to end, grace all the way down, then the only fitting response is exactly what Paul leaves us with.

Not boasting. Just gratitude. Profound, unhurried, undeserved gratitude.

When the reality of grace, unearned, undeserved, and completely finished in Christ, actually sinks in, how does that change the way you approach God, and does it free you or does some part of you still feel the pull to perform?

Where do you still find yourself trying to earn what's already been freely given? And how might today be the day that you simply receive it?

In the same way, faith by itself, if it is not accompanied by action, is dead.
James 2:17

There's no easing into James 2:17 (NIV) *"In the same way, faith by itself, if it is not accompanied by action, is dead."*

No softening. No qualifications. Dead.

James was writing to Jewish Christians scattered throughout the ancient world. These were people who knew their theology, and who could talk about faith fluently and confidently. Into that context he drops this observation: knowing the right things and saying the right things isn't enough. Faith that never shows up in how you actually live isn't faith at all.

Now, it's important to understand what James is and isn't saying here. He's not contradicting Paul's foundational teaching that salvation comes through faith and not by works. That's not the argument. What James is getting at is something else. He's describing what genuine, living faith actually looks like from the outside. And his point is straightforward: if it's real, it moves. It acts. It shows up in how you treat people, how you spend your time, how you respond to someone in need.

A tree that produces no fruit isn't resting. It's dead.

The word *dead* is deliberately blunt. Not struggling. Not immature. Not a work in progress. Dead. It's the kind of word that's meant to make you stop and honestly consider the question he's really asking.

Not *do I believe?* But *does my belief actually show?*

Think about an area of your life where your beliefs and your actions haven't quite caught up with each other yet. An area where faith is present in theory but hasn't fully shown up in practice. What is one step that might begin to close that gap?

Reflect on the question James is really asking: not whether you believe, but whether anyone around you can tell.

Have faith in God, Jesus answered. Truly I tell you, if anyone says to this mountain, 'Go, throw yourself into the sea,' and does not doubt in their heart but believes that what they say will happen, it will be done for them. Therefore I tell you, whatever you ask for in prayer, believe that you have received it, and it will be yours.
Mark 11:22-24

The context for Mark 11:22-24 (NIV) matters. The morning after Jesus cursed a fig tree, the disciples walk past it and stop in their tracks: it had withered completely, right down to the roots. Peter, never one to keep an observation to himself, points it out. And Jesus, rather than dwelling on the fig tree, uses the moment to take them somewhere much bigger.

"Have faith in God," He says. And then this:

"Truly I tell you, if anyone says to this mountain, 'Go, throw yourself into the sea,' and does not doubt in their heart but believes that what they say will happen, it will be done for them."

To anyone standing there that day, the mountain imagery would have had an immediate impact. It was a familiar expression, a way of describing something immovable, something that simply isn't going to budge by any ordinary means. Jesus is not giving a geology lesson. He's describing the kind of obstacles that make you feel stuck, the situations where human effort and resourcefulness have run out of road.

And His answer to those situations is this: *have faith in God.* Not faith in your own confidence. Not positive thinking dressed up in religious language. Faith in God: His character, His power, His faithfulness to come through.

The condition He attaches — *believing without doubting in your heart* — points to something wholehearted and undivided. A trust that has genuinely settled the question of whether God is able and whether God will act.

"Whatever you ask for in prayer, believe that you have received it, and it will be yours."

It's one of the boldest invitations in all of Scripture. Pray expectantly. Bring the mountains. Leave them with God.

What's the mountain in front of you right now? What's the thing that feels completely immovable by any ordinary means, and how do you bring it to God with the kind of faith that has genuinely settled the question of whether He is able?

And when you pray, what doubts tend to quietly show up alongside your requests? And rather than pushing them aside, what if you brought those to God too?

Patience

Be patient, then, brothers and sisters, until the Lord's coming. See how the farmer waits for the land to yield its valuable crop, patiently waiting for the autumn and spring rains. You too, be patient and stand firm, because the Lord's coming is near.
James 5:7-8

James 5:7-8 (NIV) opens with a phrase that doesn't come naturally to most of us: *"Be patient, then, brothers and sisters, until the Lord's coming."*

Patient. In the middle of hardship. In the middle of suffering and injustice and challenging seasons that seem to go on far longer than they should. Patient.

To make his point, James uses an image his audience would have known well: a farmer. A farmer doesn't plant seeds on Monday and expect a harvest by Friday. He prepares the ground, puts the seed in, and then he waits. He waits for the rain, trusting that what the soil needs will come in its proper season. He doesn't dig up the seeds every few days to check on them. He waits, not with folded arms and gritted teeth, but with the quiet, purposeful confidence of someone who knows how this works.

That's the picture James is painting. Patience, in the biblical sense, isn't passive resignation. It isn't giving up and making peace with disappointment. It's an active, expectant waiting, grounded in the absolute certainty that what has been promised is coming, and that the timing is not ours to dictate.

And then verse 8 adds something important: *"Stand firm, because the Lord's coming is near."*

Stand firm. Strengthen your heart. Keep your eyes where they belong, not on the length of the wait, but on the one who is coming.

The season is temporary. The promise is not.

Think back to a period of waiting that went longer than you thought you could bear. And looking back now, where do you see God's hand quietly at work in what felt, at the time, like silence?

And in whatever you're currently waiting on, what does "stand firm" actually mean for you, not as a general spiritual idea, but as a practical, daily choice?

Be joyful in hope, patient in affliction, faithful in prayer.
Romans 12:12

Romans 12:12 (NIV) begs a closer look. On the surface it appears deceptively simple: *"Be joyful in hope, patient in affliction, faithful in prayer."*

Three instructions. And yet there's an entire way of living packed into them.

Paul drops this verse in the middle of a rich, practical section on what the Christian life actually looks like from the inside out. And what strikes me is how these three qualities aren't presented as separate items on a checklist. They belong together. They reinforce each other. Pull one out and the others are harder to sustain.

Take *joyful in hope* first. Paul isn't describing the kind of joy that shows up on good days and disappears when things get hard. He's describing something more durable than that: a joy anchored not in how circumstances look right now, but in the certain, unshakeable promises of God that lie ahead. That kind of joy doesn't evaporate when the season turns difficult. It can't, because it isn't built on the season.

Then there's *patient in affliction.* Paul fully expects that hardship is part of the journey. He's not promising an easy road. He's calling believers to walk the difficult one without bitterness, without despair, with a steady and grace-sustained spirit that keeps putting one foot in front of the other.

And then: *faithful in prayer.* This is the foundation beneath the other two. Because the ability to remain joyful in hard seasons and patient through prolonged suffering doesn't come from trying harder. It comes from consistently bringing yourself — your hopes, your burdens, your weariness — to God in prayer.

When circumstances are hard and hope feels more like a discipline than a feeling, how do you to choose joy? And what does that joy actually anchor itself to when the easy answers aren't available?

Think back to a difficult time that, looking back, did something in you that the easier seasons simply couldn't. And what did that teach you about the unlikely gift of patience in affliction?

Therefore, as God's chosen people, holy and dearly loved, clothe yourselves with compassion, kindness, humility, gentleness and patience.
Colossians 3:12

There's an important sequence in Colossians 3. Before Paul tells believers what to put on, he tells them what to take off: the anger, the malice, the lying, the behaviors that belong to the old life. And then he says this in verse 12 (NIV):

"Therefore, as God's chosen people, holy and dearly loved, clothe yourselves with compassion, kindness, humility, gentleness and patience."

Notice what comes first, and it isn't the command. Before Paul asks anything of these believers, he tells them who they are. Chosen. Holy. Dearly loved. The instruction to clothe themselves in these virtues doesn't arrive until after their identity has been firmly established. That order is intentional.

Because if you lead with the command and skip the identity, you end up with people working their way toward compassion and kindness, trying to be patient through sheer force of will. And that works for a while, until it doesn't. Paul's approach is different. He's saying: *know who you are first. Then let that be what you dress yourself in each morning.*

The five virtues he lists — compassion, kindness, humility, gentleness, patience — paint a picture of a life genuinely turned outward toward others. Not a life consumed with protecting its own reputation or advancing its own interests, but one where grace and selfless care have taken root.

And the driver for all of it? Not willpower. Not moral resolve. Just a deep, settled understanding that you are chosen, set apart, and unconditionally loved by God.

When that sinks in, the rest follows naturally.

Think of a recent moment, maybe one that didn't feel particularly significant at the time, where you had the opportunity to show compassion, kindness, humility, gentleness, or patience. Reflect on what it did, either in you or in the person on the receiving end.

Which of those five gives you the most trouble? And rather than trying to manufacture it on your own, have you asked God to grow it in you?

Be still before the Lord and wait patiently for him; do not fret when people succeed in their ways, when they carry out their wicked schemes.

Psalm 37:7

Psalm 37:7 (NIV) addresses something that has bothered honest, God-fearing people for a very long time: *"Be still before the Lord and wait patiently for him; do not fret when people succeed in their ways, when they carry out their wicked schemes."*

David wrote the whole of Psalm 37 wrestling with a question that still feels current: why do people who disregard God seem to get ahead, while those who are trying to live faithfully face hardship and delay? It's an age-old question. It's also a very human one. And this verse gets right to the heart of his answer.

Be still. Two words that are considerably easier to read than to practice. In the original Hebrew, the idea carries the sense of releasing, of letting go of the tension, the striving, the compulsive need to fix things or force an outcome. It's not passivity exactly. It's more like the deliberate unclenching of a fist that's been gripped too tight for too long.

And then: *wait patiently.* Which adds a time dimension that most of us would rather skip. God's justice, David is telling us, doesn't always arrive on our preferred timetable. The scales don't always balance by Friday. But, ultimately, they will balance. God's timing isn't our timing, but it is never accidentally late.

Do not fret. Don't let the apparent success of those who are cutting corners pull you into anxiety or resentment. That's a trap, and David knows it.

The invitation here is a simple but demanding one: trade the fretting for stillness, and the striving for patient trust. It's not easy. But it's the path to a peace that the fretting never delivers.

In the middle of a life that rarely slows down on its own, how could you practice being still before the Lord, not as a concept, but as a practiced, deliberate part of your day?

And when someone around you seems to be getting ahead easily, fairly or otherwise, where does your heart go, and how could you trade that frustration for the quiet, steadying peace of trusting God's timing instead?

Generosity

Remember this: Whoever sows sparingly will also reap sparingly, and whoever sows generously will also reap generously. Each of you should give what you have decided in your heart to give, not reluctantly or under compulsion, for God loves a cheerful giver.
2 Corinthians 9:6-7

Paul opens 2 Corinthians 9:6-7 (NIV) with a principle that anyone who has ever planted anything will recognize: *"Whoever sows sparingly will also reap sparingly, and whoever sows generously will also reap generously."*

It's farming logic. And it's also, Paul is telling us, the logic of generosity.

Paul is writing to the church at Corinth, encouraging them to follow through on a financial commitment they'd made to support struggling believers in Jerusalem. So this isn't abstract theology, it's practical, specific, and aimed at people who needed a gentle nudge to do what they'd already said they would do.

But what Paul does with that nudge is remarkable. He takes what could have been a straightforward fundraising appeal and turns it into a window onto something much larger: the way God sees generosity, and what He does with it.

The sowing and reaping metaphor is instructive precisely because a farmer doesn't experience putting seed in the ground as a loss. He experiences it as an investment. He experiences it as an investment made with confidence that the harvest is coming, that the principle governing what goes in and what comes out is reliable and overseen by something larger than himself.

That's exactly how Paul wants the Corinthians — and us — to think about giving.

And then verse 7 brings it home: *give what you have decided in your heart to give.* Not what pressure or guilt or obligation has extracted from you. What you have genuinely, freely, joyfully decided. Because, Paul says, *God loves a cheerful giver.*

Not a reluctant one. Not a compelled one. A cheerful one.

Generosity, at its best, isn't a duty to discharge. It's a joy to lean into, a faith-filled, openhanded participation in the abundant generosity of God Himself.

Think back to a time when you gave generously, maybe more than was comfortable, and reflect honestly on what that did, both in you and in the people around you.

___

___

___

___

___

___

___

___

___

___

And where do you find yourself holding back with your time, your money, your energy? Consider what's really behind it.

One person gives freely, yet gains even more; another withholds unduly, but comes to poverty. A generous person will prosper; whoever refreshes others will be refreshed.

Proverbs 11:24-25

Proverbs 11:24-25 (NIV) opens with what sounds, on the surface, like a contradiction: "One person gives freely, yet gains even more; another withholds unduly, but comes to poverty."

Let's read that again slowly. The one who gives freely *gains more*. The one who holds tightly *ends up with less*. By any conventional measure of how wealth works, that makes no sense at all. And I think that's the point.

Solomon, for all his wisdom, wasn't naive about human nature. He knew the instinct to hold on, to accumulate, to protect, to make sure there's enough left over before you consider giving any of it away. It's deeply wired into most of us. And yet here he is, in two short verses, turning that instinct completely upside down.

Verse 25 continues: *"A generous person will prosper; whoever refreshes others will be refreshed."*

There's a beautiful reciprocity in that second line that really resonates. Whoever *refreshes* others will be *refreshed*. It's not a transaction, it's more like a cycle. Generosity set in motion has a way of coming back around, often in ways you didn't expect and couldn't have engineered on your own.

Now, this isn't a promise that generous people will necessarily become wealthy in the way the world measures wealth. It runs deeper than that. Solomon is describing a kind of abundance — of soul, of relationship, of life — that the tight-fisted accumulator never quite seems to find, no matter how much they manage to hold onto.

The open hand, it turns out, receives more than the closed one ever does.

After all, you can't refresh others with a fist.

Reflect on a time when you gave freely and something came back to you, unexpected, unplanned, and better than anything you could have arranged on your own.

And looking at your life more broadly, where has an open hand produced a richness — in relationships, in doors opened, in ways that matter — that a closed one never could have?

Give, and it will be given to you. A good measure, pressed down, shaken together and running over, will be poured into your lap. For with the measure you use, it will be measured to you.

Luke 6:38

Jesus had a gift for reaching into everyday life and pulling out an image that made a point unforgettable. Luke 6:38 (NIV) is a perfect example:

"Give, and it will be given to you: A good measure, pressed down, shaken together and filled to overflowing, will be poured into your lap; for with the measure you use, it will be measured to you."

Anyone in His audience who had ever visited a market stall would have known exactly what He was describing. When a merchant measured out grain, there was a minimum way to do it: fill the container, level it off, hand it over. And then there was the generous way. Press it down, shake it together to settle everything, and keep filling until it's spilling over the top. Same container. Completely different spirit.

That's the image Jesus reaches for when He talks about how God responds to a generous life.

And then there's the phrase: *poured into your lap*. Picture someone gathering the front of their robe to carry an unexpected, overflowing load of grain they weren't quite prepared for. That's the picture of what God's response to generosity looks like. Not measured out to the minimum. Not carefully rationed. Pressed down, shaken together, overflowing, and more than you can comfortably carry.

Jesus spoke these words during the Sermon on the Plain, in the middle of a broader teaching on love, mercy, and how the postures we extend toward others have a way of shaping what comes back to us. The principle cuts both ways: *with the measure you use, it will be measured to you.* Generous measure out, generous measure back.

It's one of the most liberating invitations in all of Scripture. Generosity, in Jesus' hands, is never ultimately a loss. It's a seed planted in the most reliable soil there is. The boundless, overflowing generosity of God Himself.

Give freely. Leave the measuring to Him.

When you think about the principle that the measure you use will be measured back to you, how could that manifest in the everyday — in how you give your time, your attention, your resources, your grace toward others?

When you give, what's really driving it? Genuine love and gratitude, a quiet expectation of something in return, or something else you haven't quite identified?

In everything I did, I showed you that by this kind of hard work we must help the weak, remembering the words the Lord Jesus himself said: 'It is more blessed to give than to receive.'
Acts 20:35

There's something to consider here before we even get to the words themselves. Acts 20:35 (NIV) records Paul quoting Jesus directly: *"It is more blessed to give than to receive"*. And here's what makes that remarkable: this saying of Jesus appears nowhere in Matthew, Mark, Luke, or John. Not one of the four Gospels. This is the only place in the entire New Testament where it's recorded.

Which means Paul had it. He'd carried it. And at this particular moment — his farewell address to the elders of the church at Ephesus, a deeply personal and emotionally charged goodbye — he chose to bring it out.

The setting matters. Paul isn't delivering this from a position of comfort or success. He's a man who has worked with his own hands to support himself and those around him, who has poured himself out in service to others across years of travel, hardship, and opposition. When he quotes Jesus saying it is more blessed to give than to receive, he's not offering a pleasant sentiment. He's describing the life he has actually lived.

That word *blessed* carries a lot of weight here. It speaks to a deep, lasting happiness. An inner flourishing and sense of divine favor that goes well beyond the momentary pleasure of acquiring something new.

Paul is pointing to a joy that accumulation simply cannot produce, no matter how much is accumulated.

And the verse itself has the quality of something that's been refined down to its essence. Simple enough to remember. Yet deep enough to consider.

Because if we're honest, the pull toward receiving rather than giving is strong and constant. It's the default setting for most of us. And yet here is Jesus, preserved in Paul's farewell address to people he loves, quietly insisting that we have it backwards.

The greater blessing, it turns out, is on the other side of the open hand.

Jesus didn't say it is *equally* blessed to give, He said *more* blessed. Where have you actually experienced that to be true in your own life?

___

___

___

___

___

___

___

___

___

___

___

And today, what is one thing you could give, whether it's time, encouragement, resources, or simply your full attention to someone who needs it?

Kindness

Be kind and compassionate to one another, forgiving each other, just as in Christ God forgave you.
Ephesians 4:32

Ephesians 4:32 (NIV) is one of those verses that reads simply on the surface but carries a significant amount of weight underneath: *"Be kind and compassionate to one another, forgiving each other, just as in Christ God forgave you."*

Three qualities. One sentence. And a standard that gets right to the heart of what Christian relationships are actually supposed to look like.

Paul has spent the earlier part of this chapter calling believers to put away the behaviors of the old life: bitterness, rage, anger, slander. And this verse arrives as the positive counterpart to all of that. Not just *stop doing this,* but *start doing this instead*. Kindness. Compassion. Forgiveness. The wardrobe of the new self, you might say.

And each of those qualities runs counter to what comes naturally when we've been hurt, overlooked, or treated unfairly. Kindness is easy when people are kind to us. Compassion flows freely when we're not the ones who've been wronged. Forgiveness — real forgiveness, not just the polite surface variety — is one of the hardest things any of us will ever be asked to practice.

Which is exactly why Paul doesn't simply say do these things, then leaves us to find the motivation on our own. He gives us the source that drives all three: *just as in Christ God forgave you.*

That phrase changes everything. It shifts the foundation from personal effort and moral resolve, to something that never runs out. The experience of having been forgiven a debt we could never have repaid, by a grace we did nothing to deserve.

When that reality is kept close and reflected on regularly, kindness, compassion, and forgiveness stop feeling like obligations and start feeling like the most natural response in the world.

After all, it's hard to withhold from others what you know has been so freely given to you.

Think back to a time when forgiveness felt genuinely difficult, when everything in you resisted it. Then ask yourself honestly how the reality of what God has already forgiven in you inspired you to extend it to someone else.

____

____

____

____

____

____

____

____

____

____

And this week, in the relationships closest to you, how might kindness and compassion show up not as grand gestures but as small, deliberate, everyday choices?

Those who are kind benefit themselves, but the cruel bring ruin on themselves.
Proverbs 11:17

Solomon had a gift for saying something profound in the fewest possible words, and Proverbs 11:17 (NIV) is a good example: *"Those who are kind benefit themselves, but the cruel bring ruin on themselves."*

No preamble. No lengthy explanation. Just a clean, direct observation about cause and effect — the kind that makes you stop and think because you recognize it's true.

What strikes me about this verse is its honesty about self-interest. Solomon isn't appealing to some lofty, purely altruistic motivation for kindness. He's making a more straightforward and persuasive case: how you treat other people has a way of coming back to you. Be kind, and you benefit yourself. Be cruel, and you bring ruin on yourself. It's not complicated.

The word *benefit* in the first half carries the sense of genuine flourishing, not just a warm feeling after doing something nice, but a real enrichment of soul, relationship, and life that accumulates in a person who has made kindness their habitual way of moving through the world. There's something that grows in the kind person that simply doesn't grow in the unkind one.

And then the second half arrives with force. The cruel *bring ruin on themselves*. Not on others, on themselves. Whatever damage harshness and cruelty do to the people on the receiving end, Solomon is pointing out that the person practicing it pays a price too. Something erodes. Something is lost that doesn't easily come back.

It's a verse worth reflecting on. Not asking whether we consider ourselves cruel, most of us don't, but asking the quieter question: what is my habitual posture toward the people around me?

Kindness, it turns out, is never wasted. Not even on yourself.

Think of a time when a simple act of kindness turned out to benefit you just as much as the person on the receiving end. What did that teach you about how generosity of spirit tends to work?

And looking at your life or the community around you, where have you seen kindness quietly compound over time, producing something richer and more lasting than anyone expected?

But the fruit of the Spirit is love, joy, peace, forbearance, kindness, goodness, faithfulness, gentleness and self-control. Against such things there is no law.
Galatians 5:22-23

Galatians 5:22-23 (NIV) is one of those passages that most believers could recite from memory: *"But the fruit of the Spirit is love, joy, peace, forbearance, kindness, goodness, faithfulness, gentleness and self-control. Against such things there is no law."*

Nine qualities. One word to describe them all: *fruit.*

That choice of word is deliberate. Paul doesn't say the *works* of the Spirit, or the *disciplines* of the Spirit, or the *achievements* of the Spirit. He says fruit. And anyone who has ever grown anything knows that fruit is not manufactured, it's produced. It grows naturally and inevitably from a healthy root and a good source of nourishment. You don't grit your teeth and produce an apple. You tend the tree, keep it connected to what it needs, and the fruit comes.

That's exactly the picture Paul is painting of the Christian life. Love, joy, peace, forbearance, kindness, goodness, faithfulness, gentleness, self-control. These aren't a checklist of virtues to be developed one at a time through sheer force of will. They are the natural outgrowth of a life genuinely surrendered to and inhabited by the Holy Spirit.

It's also noteworthy that Paul uses the singular: fruit, not *fruits.* These nine qualities aren't a menu to pick and choose from, taking the ones that come naturally and quietly skipping the harder ones. They form a whole. The Spirit's work in a life tends to produce all of them together, as a unified expression of Christ-like character growing from the inside out.

And then the closing verse: *against such things there is no law.* That carries a quiet note of triumph. A life shaped by the

Spirit doesn't need an external law to keep it in check. It has already been transformed at the source.

That's not willpower. That's grace doing what grace does best.

Of the nine — love, joy, peace, forbearance, kindness, goodness, faithfulness, gentleness, self-control — which one do you see most clearly in your life right now, and which one still has the most growing to do?

And here's the important reminder that goes with that: these are fruit, not achievements. So, rather than trying harder, where might you need to simply stay more connected to the vine and trust the Spirit to do what only the Spirit can do?

Trust

Trust in the Lord with all your heart and lean not on your own understanding; in all your ways submit to him, and he will make your paths straight.
Proverbs 3:5-6

If there's a verse that has found its way onto more wall art, greeting cards, and graduation gifts than almost any other, it's probably Proverbs 3:5-6 (NIV): *"Trust in the Lord with all your heart and lean not on your own understanding; in all your ways submit to him, and he will make your paths straight."*

Solomon wrote this as guidance to his son — practical, fatherly wisdom about how to navigate life well. And the counsel he offers isn't complicated. But it is demanding.

Trust in the Lord with all your heart. Not most of your heart. Not the parts that don't have a better plan. All of it. Every corner, every worry, every ambition, every fear. The standard Solomon sets here is total, and that totality is exactly what makes it challenging, because most of us are quite comfortable trusting God with some things while quietly retaining management of others.

Lean not on your own understanding. This one runs counter to a human nature that prizes independence, self-sufficiency, and the confidence of having figured things out on your own. Solomon isn't saying stop thinking. He's saying stop making your own reasoning the final authority.

In all your ways submit to him. Not just the big decisions. Not just the crossroads moments when you genuinely don't know which way to turn. All your ways: the ordinary days, the routine choice, the small direction that quietly shapes where you end up.

And the promise attached to all of this? *He will make your paths straight.*

Not easy, necessarily. But clear. Purposeful. Guided by a hand that knows where you're going far better than you do.

It's a verse that sounds simple until you actually try to live it. And then it becomes a daily practice, and a daily gift.

This week, in the decisions both big and small, how could you genuinely submit your plans to God before moving forward, not as a formality, but as a real, trusting act of dependence?

___

___

___

___

___

___

___

___

___

___

___

___

And when you think about God making your paths straight, what does that actually mean for you? Not a life without difficulty, but something better and more reliable than that?

When I am afraid, I put my trust in you. In God, whose word I praise— in God I trust and am not afraid. What can mere mortals do to me?

Psalm 56:3-4

Psalm 56:3-4 (NIV) doesn't open with a triumphant declaration. It opens with an admission: *"When I am afraid."*

Words that immediately tell you this is someone writing from real life. David wrote this psalm after being seized by the Philistines in Gath — caught, vulnerable, surrounded by people who had every reason to want him dead. This isn't poetic fear. This is genuine.

And what makes the psalm so enduring is precisely that honesty. David doesn't pretend the fear isn't there. He doesn't open with a confident declaration and skip over the difficulty to get to the good part. He starts exactly where he is: afraid.

When I am afraid, I put my trust in you.

The word *when* matters. Not *if* I am ever afraid, as though fear were some unlikely visitor that a person of sufficient faith would never encounter. *When*. Because fear shows up. It shows up for David. It shows up for all of us. The question isn't whether we'll ever be afraid. The question is what we do with it when it arrives.

And David's answer is this: I redirect it. I take the fear and I point it toward God rather than letting it spiral into despair or paralysis. It's a deliberate choice, not a feeling that washes over him, but a decision he makes.

In God I trust and am not afraid. David is speaking truth to his own trembling heart, anchoring again to what he knows to be solid when everything else feels uncertain.

And then the closing verse, almost defiant in its simplicity:
What can mere mortals do to me?

Not a boast. A perspective. When God is the fixed point, everything else finds its actual, much smaller, size.

Think back to a time when fear had a genuine grip on you, not a minor worry, but the real thing. Reflect on what trusting God looked like in that moment and what it made possible that fear alone never could have.

____

____

____

____

____

____

____

____

____

____

____

____

____

____

What are one or two things you can put in place — a verse, a habit, a conversation, a moment of stillness — to remind yourself, when fear shows up again, that what you're trusting in is infinitely greater than what you're afraid of?

But blessed is the one who trusts in the Lord, whose confidence is in him. They will be like a tree planted by the water that sends out its roots by the stream. It does not fear when heat comes; its leaves are always green. It has no worries in a year of drought and never fails to bear fruit.

Jeremiah 17:7-8

Jeremiah 17:7-8 (NIV) arrives with words that signal something good is coming: "But blessed is the one who trusts in the Lord, whose confidence is in him."

Just a few verses earlier, Jeremiah painted a bleak picture of what life looks like for those who place their ultimate confidence in human strength and turn their hearts away from God: parched, fruitless, inhabiting a desert of their own making.

Then, *blessed*. And this:

"They will be like a tree planted by the water that sends out its roots by the stream. It does not fear when heat comes; its leaves are always green. It has no worries in a year of drought and never fails to bear fruit."

This is an impactful image. The tree planted by the stream isn't exempt from heat. It isn't sheltered from drought. The hard seasons still come, they come for everyone. But this tree has something the others don't: roots that have grown down deep into a source of nourishment that the drought simply cannot reach. While every other tree around it is struggling and withering, this one's leaves are still green. It's still bearing fruit.

That's not luck. That's roots.

And Jeremiah is telling us that this is what trust in God actually looks like in a human life. Not a life without difficulty or heat or long dry seasons. But a life so deeply and continuously nourished by its connection to God that external conditions lose their power to wither it.

Leaves always green. Fruit that never fails. Not because the circumstances are always favorable, but because the root goes somewhere the drought can't follow.

That's the promise. And it's a good one to remember, especially in the dry seasons.

When you assess where your roots are drawing their nourishment from right now, how deep do they go? When a difficult season hits, do you find yourself staying green or beginning to wither?

In the dry seasons, the ones where God feels distant and the wait feels endless, what practices, habits, or truths help you stay connected to the stream?

Humility

Do nothing out of selfish ambition or vain conceit. Rather, in humility value others above yourselves, not looking to your own interests but each of you to the interests of the others.
Philippians 2:3-4

Paul doesn't ease us into Philippians 2:3-4 (NIV). He opens with a flat prohibition: *"Do nothing out of selfish ambition or vain conceit."*

Nothing. It's the same sweeping standard he used in Philippians 4:6 with anxiety: not *less,* not *try to minimize,* but *nothing.*

Paul wrote this to the believers at Philippi, a church he genuinely loved, in the middle of a passionate appeal for unity. And what he identifies as the primary enemies of that unity are revealing: selfish ambition and vain conceit. Two relatives, but worth distinguishing. Selfish ambition is the driven pursuit of personal advancement and getting ahead, even if it means others get left behind. Vain conceit is the hunger for recognition, the need to be seen as significant and it can poison relationships from the inside.

Both of them, Paul is saying, have to go.

And what replaces them? *"In humility value others above yourselves, not looking to your own interests but each of you to the interests of the others."*

Paul is not asking anyone to pretend their own needs don't exist. The call to value others above yourself is a reorientation of the heart's default posture, a shift from instinctively centering every situation on yourself to asking what the person in front of you actually needs.

It's a significant ask. And Paul knows it. Which is why, in the very next verses, he points to the only example big enough to ground it: a Savior who laid aside everything, not for His own interests, but for ours.

Humility, in the end, isn't something we work up. It's something we catch, from a long, honest look at Christ.

Think of a time when you chose someone else's interests over your own. Maybe it came naturally, maybe it cost you something. Reflect honestly on what it felt like and what it quietly taught you.

Where does selfish ambition or pride still have a foothold in your life? And have you invited God into those areas?

But he gives us more grace. That is why Scripture says: "God opposes the proud but shows favor to the humble."
James 4:6

James 4:6 (NIV) opens with: *"But he gives us more grace."*

More grace. Not a fixed, limited supply that runs out when you've drawn on it too many times. Not grace that gets harder to access the more you've needed it. More grace, as in, whatever the need, whatever the failure, whatever the gap between where you are and where you ought to be, God's grace is always greater still.

That's the opening. And it sets up everything that follows.

"That is why Scripture says: 'God opposes the proud but shows favor to the humble.'"

James draws a contrast here. On one side, the humble, receiving favor. On the other, the proud, met with something impactful. Not indifference. Not gentle correction. *Opposition*. God actively placing Himself in resistance to the proud heart.

Pride, at its core, is the posture that says: *I've got this. I don't need help. I can manage on my own.* And into that posture, God brings resistance. Not because He is harsh, but because pride is a closed door, and grace requires an open one.

Humility, on the other hand, is simply the honest acknowledgment that we can't, that we need, that we are dependent. And to that posture, God brings favor, and more grace than we know what to do with.

The invitation here is both a warning and a relief. Stop trying to manage life on your own terms.

Open your hands and discover that the grace waiting there is more than enough for whatever you're carrying.

Reflect on a time when pride quietly put distance between you and God, or between you and someone you cared about. Where did grace show up in that situation, even when you didn't necessarily deserve it?

What does receiving God's favor through humility actually mean for you in practice, as a lived, daily reality?

In the same way, you who are younger, submit yourselves to your elders. All of you, clothe yourselves with humility toward one another, because, God opposes the proud but shows favor to the humble. Humble yourselves, therefore, under God's mighty hand, that he may lift you up in due time.

1 Peter 5:5-6

1 Peter 5:5-6 (NIV) brings together two dimensions of humility that are easy to treat separately but belong together. First, humility toward one another. Then, humility before God.

"All of you, clothe yourselves with humility toward one another, because 'God opposes the proud but shows favor to the humble.' Humble yourselves, therefore, under God's mighty hand, that he may lift you up in due time."

Peter was writing to younger believers who were navigating real suffering, the kind that comes from being marginalized, misunderstood, and living as outsiders in a world that wasn't particularly friendly toward them. And into that context, his counsel is this: humility. Toward each other, and before God.

The clothing metaphor again: *clothe yourselves with humility.* We saw it in Colossians 3, and here it is again. And the repetition across different writers tells us something. Humility isn't a personality trait that some people are fortunate enough to be born with. It's a garment. Something you make a deliberate choice to put on, every day, in your dealings with the people around you.

Peter then quotes the same verse from Proverbs that James did — *God opposes the proud but shows favor to the humble* — which tells us this wasn't an obscure text in the early church.

It was a cornerstone. A truth they kept coming back to because it kept proving itself true.

And then verse 6 adds something that I find remarkable. *Humble yourselves under God's mighty hand, that he may lift you up in due time.*

The same hand that is mighty enough to lift you up is the hand you are being asked to humble yourself under. Peter is saying trust it. Surrender to it. Stop working to engineer your own elevation and place yourself, quietly and completely, in hands that are more than capable of raising you up at exactly the right moment.

In due time. Not your time. His.

That's the promise, and it's worth the wait.

Think about the person or relationship where humility comes hardest and where submission feels most challenging. Ask yourself what God might be doing in you through that friction.

____

____

____

____

____

____

____

____

In the ordinary interactions of your day, the ones that don't feel particularly significant, how could you deliberately put humility on?

Joy

Do not grieve, for the joy of the Lord is your strength.
Nehemiah 8:10

The setting for Nehemiah 8:10 (NIV) is important to know, because it provides a context that helps you understand what's happening.

The Israelites have returned from Babylonian exile. The walls of Jerusalem have been rebuilt, a remarkable achievement in itself. And now the people have gathered in the square to hear Ezra read aloud from the Book of the Law of Moses. Some of them, perhaps, are hearing it for the first time. And as the crowd listens, something happens. They begin to weep.

It's a genuine moment, the kind of communal grief that comes from a people suddenly confronted with the distance between who they have been and who God called them to be. Real conviction. Real sorrow. The kind that doesn't need to be manufactured or talked into.

And into that moment, Nehemiah speaks: *"Do not grieve, for the joy of the Lord is your strength."*

He doesn't dismiss the grief or tell the people they're overreacting. He acknowledges it — and then redirects it. Because this day, he says, is holy. It's a day for feasting and celebration and sharing with those who have nothing. The grief has done its work. Now comes something better.

The joy of the Lord is your strength.

Not your own joy, manufactured on a good day when things are going well. The joy of the Lord: something given, sustained, and sourced entirely in God Himself. A joy that remains when circumstances are hard or when you've fallen short again. A joy rooted not in your performance but in His presence and His unfailing love toward you.

That's what Nehemiah is pointing these weeping people toward. Not guilt. Not self-improvement. Not trying harder next time.

Just this: come back to the joy. It's where your strength has been all along.

During difficult times when your own reserves are running low, what does it mean for you to draw strength from the joy of the Lord rather than from what you can manifest on your own?

____

____

____

____

____

____

____

____

____

____

____

____

Think of something you're working through right now, or recently came through, and ask yourself: where was God's joy available to you in that, and did you receive it?

You make known to me the path of life; you will fill me with joy in your presence, with eternal pleasures at your right hand.

Psalm 16:11

Psalm 16:11 (NIV) is the final note of a psalm that has been building toward it all along: *"You make known to me the path of life; you will fill me with joy in your presence, with eternal pleasures at your right hand."*

By the time David reaches this verse, he has already declared the Lord his refuge, his inheritance, his portion, his counselor — the one in whom every good thing is found. And now, in this closing line, all of that comes together in a single, statement about what life in God's presence actually looks like.

You make known to me the path of life.

Not just any path, the path of life. David doesn't say God assists him along a path he's already chosen, or shows up when he's gone the wrong way and needs redirecting. God makes it known. He reveals it. He goes ahead of it. The implication is clear enough: apart from His leading, the fullness of life that we were made for remains somewhere just out of reach, undiscovered.

And then: *you will fill me with joy in your presence.*

Fill. Not provide a modest, adequate supply of. *Fill*. There's an abundance in that word. David is describing a joy that goes all the way down, not the surface happiness that shows up on good days and disappears when things get hard, but a deep, soul-level satisfaction that is uniquely and inexhaustibly available in one place.

In God's presence.

With eternal pleasures at your right hand. Eternal, meaning these pleasures don't expire, don't diminish, don't eventually disappoint the way so many other things do. They are at His right hand, the place of honor, of being close to the one who holds everything.

David is telling us the direction we're looking for, the joy we're hungry for, the pleasure we keep chasing in a dozen different directions — it's all here. In His presence. At His right hand.

And it turns out, that's exactly where we were meant to be all along.

Looking back over your life, where do you most clearly see God revealing the path: a decision, a redirection, a door that opened or closed at exactly the right moment? And what did His presence feel like in that?

Think of a moment when spiritual joy caught you off guard, when God's nearness was simply undeniable. What was happening, and what did it tell you about where true joy actually comes from?

I have told you this so that my joy may be in you and that your joy may be complete.
John 15:11

The timing of John 15:11 (NIV) impacts me every time I read it.

Jesus is in the upper room. It's the night of His betrayal. Within hours, He will be arrested, tried, and crucified. He knows exactly what is coming, every detail. And yet, in this moment, what He is focused on is not His own suffering. It's the joy of the people sitting around the table with Him.

"I have told you this so that my joy may be in you and that your joy may be complete."

This is the purpose statement for everything He has just taught them about the vine and the branches: the abiding, the keeping of His commandments, the remaining in His love. All of it, He says, has been leading here. Not to their theological correctness. Not simply to their obedience. To their *joy*.

And look at the kind of joy He's talking about. *My joy* — the joy that belongs to Jesus Himself, rooted in His perfect, unbroken relationship with the Father. He's not offering His followers a lesser version of what He has. He's inviting them into the same joy that sustains Him. The same deep, settled, unshakeable joy that no circumstance, not even the cross, can touch.

And the standard He sets? *Complete.* Not partial. Not fragile. Not the kind that requires everything to be going well in order to survive. Full. Whole. Overflowing.

That your joy may be complete.

I find that both humbling and extraordinary. On the night when Jesus had every reason to be consumed with what was coming for Him, His concern was this — that the people He loved would know a joy so full and so deeply rooted in Him that nothing the world could do would be able to take it away.

That's not a teacher giving a lesson. That's a Savior revealing His heart.

When you think about what complete joy, the kind Jesus is talking about, rooted in Him and unshaken by circumstances, how close does your daily experience come to that, and where are the gaps?

____

____

____

____

____

____

____

____

____

____

____

____

____

And what does remaining connected to Christ mean for you today, not as a religious routine, but as the kind of living, abiding connection that keeps the joy flowing?

May the God of hope fill you with all joy and peace as you trust in him, so that you may overflow with hope by the power of the Holy Spirit.
Romans 15:13

Romans 15:13 (NIV) is one of those verses that functions as both a prayer and a promise: *"May the God of hope fill you with all joy and peace as you trust in him, so that you may overflow with hope by the power of the Holy Spirit."*

Paul is near the end of his letter to the Romans, a letter that has covered extraordinary theological ground, and he closes this section with a benediction. A blessing spoken over a community that has just been called to something difficult: welcoming one another across significant cultural and religious divides, bearing with each other's differences, and building something unified out of what was, humanly speaking, unlikely material.

And the blessing he offers them for that task is this. Joy. Peace. Hope. Overflowing.

Paul calls God the *God of hope* here. Not simply a God who occasionally provides hope, or who offers hope as one of many available features. Hope is woven into who He is. It's an attribute, as fundamental to His nature as His love or His faithfulness. Which means that hope, for the believer, is never dependent on how things look at any given moment. It flows from a source that circumstances simply cannot reach.

And then Paul asks that they be *filled* with joy and peace, right to the brim, nothing held back. But he doesn't stop there. The filling leads to *overflowing*. What God pours in becomes too much to contain within a single life, and it spills outward, into relationships, into community, into the lives of people around them.

That overflow, Paul says, happens *by the power of the Holy Spirit*. Not by trying harder. Not by getting everything right. By the Spirit doing what only the Spirit can do.

It's a clear vision of what a life and a community look like when it has been genuinely filled by the God of hope.

Not just enough to get by. Overflowing.

Where have you seen trust in God produce a joy and peace in your life that your own effort and planning simply couldn't have generated? And where are you still holding the reins a little tighter than you need to?

And what is one practical step you can take this week to loosen that grip, to open your hands a little wider and let God do what only He can do?

Hope

For I know the plans I have for you, declares the Lord, plans to prosper you and not to harm you, plans to give you hope and a future.
Jeremiah 29:11

Jeremiah 29:11 in the NIV may be one of the most quoted verses in all of scripture: *"'For I know the plans I have for you,' declares the Lord, 'plans to prosper you and not to harm you, plans to give you hope and a future.'"*

God spoke these words through Jeremiah to the Israelites living in Babylonian exile. They weren't in a difficult season that was about to turn around in a few weeks. They were displaced, far from home, far from their temple, far from everything familiar, and they would be for a generation. This wasn't a promise of immediate rescue. It was something to hold onto during a long and painful wait.

"I know the plans I have for you." In the middle of exile, when everything looked like abandonment, when God's silence might easily have been mistaken for absence, He says this. I know and I have plans. This is not out of my hands. Your suffering exists within a purpose I am overseeing, even when you cannot see it from where you're currently at.

And then a contrast. Plans *to prosper* and *not to harm*. It's a gentle but deliberate pushback against the very human tendency to interpret hardship as evidence that God is against us. He isn't. His intentions toward His people are good, purposeful, and moving, even through the long and difficult times, toward something that deserves to be called hope and a future.

Jeremiah 29:11 doesn't promise that the road will be short or easy. It promises something better. It promises that the one who holds the future is the same one who holds His people, and that His plans for them are worth trusting, even when, and especially when, the wait is long.

Think back to a time when God's plans made no sense from where you were at, when trust felt more like a risk than a comfort. And looking back now, where do you see His guidance or provision quietly at work in what felt like uncertainty?

And when you read that His plans are to give you hope and a future — not harm, not abandonment, but genuine hope — what does that mean for the struggles you're facing right now?

May the God of hope fill you with all joy and peace as you trust in him, so that you may overflow with hope by the power of the Holy Spirit.

Romans 15:13

Romans 15:13 (NIV) is a verse I comeback to regularly. *"May the God of hope fill you with all joy and peace as you trust in him, so that you may overflow with hope by the power of the Holy Spirit."*

Paul is wrapping up a section of his letter to the Romans in which he's been calling a diverse, sometimes divided community to receive one another, bear with one another, and build something together that none of them could manage on their own. And this is the blessing he speaks to them.

God of hope. Paul doesn't say God, who occasionally provides hope, or God who offers hope among other things. He says God of hope, as if hope is woven into the very fabric of who He is. Which means the hope Paul is talking about here isn't something we generate through positive thinking or favorable circumstances. It flows from a source entirely outside of us, from a God whose nature is hope itself.

And then the progression. *As you trust in him*. Here's the condition, and it's a simple one. Not as you perform well enough, or as you have everything figured out, but as you trust. That's the channel through which everything else flows.

Trust opens the door to being *filled*: with joy, with peace. All of it. And then the filling leads to *overflowing*. What God pours into a life that trusts Him cannot be contained within that single life. It spills out. It reaches the people nearby. It shapes the community around it.

By the power of the Holy Spirit. Not by effort. Not by trying to be more hopeful. By the Holy Spirit.

It's a prayer worth praying for yourself. And for the people you love.

May you overflow.

Where have you experienced God's hope, joy, or peace most tangibly in your life? And where are you still holding something back that you haven't quite surrendered to Him yet?

And how could you let that hope overflow into your relationships, your community, the people closest to you — by simply staying open to what the Holy Spirit wants to do?

Why, my soul, are you downcast? Why so disturbed within me? Put your hope in God, for I will yet praise him, my Savior.
Psalm 42:11

Psalm 42:11 (NIV) doesn't open with a declaration of triumph. It opens with two questions directed not at God or at anyone else, but inward: *"Why, my soul, are you downcast? Why so disturbed within me?"*

It's one of the most honest declarations, and one of the most relatable.

The psalm was written by the Sons of Korah during a season of real isolation and inner turmoil — a deep, aching longing for God's presence that wasn't being met in the ways the writer had known before. The pain is genuine. The disorientation is genuine. And the psalmist puts it on the page exactly as it feels.

He doesn't simply sit inside the despair and let it have the final word. He steps back from it. He addresses his own soul, almost as if pulling himself aside for a quiet conversation, and interrogates what's happening rather than being swept away by it. It's a very insightful spiritual practice, and not an easy one. When emotions are running that deep, the last thing that comes naturally is to examine them with clarity.

And yet here he is, doing exactly that.
"Put your hope in God, for I will yet praise him, my Savior and my God."

Not *I praise him* — present tense, easy, when everything feels fine. *I will yet praise him,* future tense, chosen in the dark, before the feelings have caught up. It's a declaration made not because the circumstances have changed, but because the psalmist has decided, against the grain of everything he's feeling, to anchor himself to something that doesn't change.

Psalm 42:11 is a gift to anyone who has known the weight of depression, doubt, or spiritual darkness. It doesn't offer a quick fix or a simple answer. It offers something better, an honest companion who has been in that same dark place, and who found, in the choice to put his hope in God, a way through.

Not around. Through.

Think back to a time when you were consumed with discouragement and when praise felt like the last thing that came naturally. How did you find your way back to hope?

____

____

____

____

____

____

____

____

____

____

____

And in whatever difficult season you may be walking through right now, how could you follow the psalmist's example — to speak honestly to your own soul, redirect it toward God, and choose praise?

www.ingramcontent.com/pod-product-compliance
Lightning Source LLC
LaVergne TN
LVHW010838120826
845149LV00017B/3153
9798999887795